MOSER
Legacy in Wood

Thomas Moser
***with* Donna McNeil**

Down East Books
An imprint of
Rowman & Littlefield

Published by Down East Books
An imprint of The Rowman & Littlefield Publishing Group, Inc.
4501 Forbes Boulevard, Suite 200, Lanham, Maryland 20706
www.rowman.com

Unit A, Whitacre Mews, 26-34 Stannary Street, London SE11 4AB, United Kingdom

Distributed by NATIONAL BOOK NETWORK

Design by Lynda Chilton, *BooksDesigned.com*

Copyright © 2015 by Thos. Moser Cabinetmakers

All rights reserved. No part of this book may be reproduced in any form or by any electronic or mechanical means, including information storage and retrieval systems, without written permission from the publisher, except by a reviewer who may quote passages in a review.

British Library Cataloguing in Publication Information Available

Library of Congress Cataloging-in-Publication Data

Library of Congress Cataloging-in-Publication Data Available

ISBN 978-1-60893-607-6 (cloth : alk. paper)
ISBN 978-1-60893-608-3 (electronic)

∞™ The paper used in this publication meets the minimum requirements of American National Standard for Information Sciences—Permanence of Paper for Printed Library Materials, ANSI/NISO Z39.48-1992.

Printed in the United States of America

This book reflects the artistry, discipline, and commitment of the men and women who are Thos. Moser Cabinetmakers. They, along with those who administer the company, are collectively responsible for our success, which began with the efforts of Mary Moser and our four sons: Matthew, Andrew, Aaron, and David. It is to them that I dedicate this work.

Thos. Moser

Scoop Seat Stool

Capitan's Chair

Banker's Chair

Martha Washington Chair

Four small tables

Barrel Chair

CONTENTS

Foreword	*Mira Nakashima-Yarnell*	7
Prologue	Beginnings: *Donna McNeil*	11
Legacy in Wood	*Thomas Moser*	15
Chapter 1	Influences	16
Chapter 2	Aesthetics	35
Chapter 3	The Windsor Chair—Moser style	51
Chapter 4	From the Forest	63
Chapter 5	Technology and the Hand	81
Chapter 6	Creating a Community of Makers	89
Epilogue	The Five Values	133
Afterword	*Donna McNeil*	135
Appendix I	Timeline of Key Milestones	136
Appendix II	Institutional Clients	149
Further Reading		157

FOREWORD

Mira Nakashima-Yarnell

"it is an art and soul satisfying adventure to walk the forests of the world, to commune with trees. . . . To bring this living material to the work bench, ultimately to give it a second life."

George Nakashima

Thomas Moser is a first-generation furniture maker, while I am second-generation, following in the footsteps of my father, George Nakashima. Tom's parents arrived in the United States as German immigrants; my father's came from Japan. Both sets of our parents were dedicated to the hard work of making a living in a new country, values that were instilled in George Nakashima and Tom Moser. These values served them well when they eventually reached a stage in their lives when the education they had received and careers they'd begun no longer fulfilled them, and they charted their own paths of hard work and fortitude. Consequently, in different ways and in different times they both turned to craftsmanship in wood as a way of protesting the vicissitudes of modern civilization. My father proudly called himself "the world's first hippie," and Tom's first shop was populated by men who had given up careers that "normal" education had afforded them to search for something more real than intellectual gamesmanship, pushing papers, and making phantom money. Like the

Arts and Crafts movement of the nineteenth and twentieth centuries, each man resolved to fulfill themselves by working honestly with real wood, real tools, and their own hands. George and Tom became friends and Tom always looked to George as a role model.

Both Tom and my father chose perfect women to be their life and business partners—women who were willing to endure hardship for the love of work and family in order to make the furniture-making ventures bloom and prosper. Mary Moser and Marion Nakashima were for many years the entire office staff of their respective family businesses, managing the essentials of successful enterprises: publicity, marketing, payroll, and balancing the books, in addition to raising families and helping to build their homes.

Tom and George were similarly rooted in the Shaker tradition of honesty, utilitarianism, and simplicity. They worked, as Mother Ann said, "as if you had a thousand years to live and as if you were to die tomorrow," eschewing decoration of any sort other than what the trees themselves offered. Where my father adopted the spirit of the Shakers, Tom followed their forms and methods of construction. They were both also influenced by Japanese design; my father obviously had deep roots and experience in that aesthetic, while Tom's admiration eventually informed his designs more obliquely.

My father's early furniture designs were very simple and rectilinear, based on a keen sense of structural proportion acquired during his years as a practicing architect and shaped by apprenticing to a Japanese carpenter during our wartime incarceration. Nakashima had a very artistic hand from an early age, but his way of being was infused with the spiritual experience of the Sri Aurobindo Ashram in India in the 1930s. His use of "free-form" slabs, which made him famous, was founded largely on economic necessity and inspired by Japanese tradition, a richly creative imagination, and first-hand knowledge of Japanese woodworking techniques.

Turning away from a tenured professorship in rhetoric, Tom Moser learned his craft by deconstructing and reconstructing existent furniture, then reinventing it through his reductive aesthetic as he came into his own as a maker of fine furniture. Tom Moser also understands fine craft as a spiritual endeavor and infuses his objects with his own sense of grace and form that align with functionality.

Both Tom and I have travelled far on a clear path for about the same number of years. We are perched on the brink of deciding what to do when we are no longer able to be in the workshop every day. We both hope that our work, our ethics, and our aesthetic sensibilities will continue on through at least another generation, that there will be enough trees sustainably harvested to supply our industry, and enough people who love wood and are dedicated to working with their hands. We feel an obligation to keep the spirit of true craft traditions alive and well as long as we can, and that building honest and utilitarian "antiques of the future" is an intimidating yet important vocation.

PROLOGUE

Beginnings: *Donna McNeil*

From the earliest moment and throughout his life, Thomas Moser had a compulsion to build, to create something real and physical with his hands. This activity was constant. As Tom tells it, "To this day I cannot imagine a life in which I am not creating objects in three dimensions. The urge runs deep in my bones, and for better or worse, I define myself by my output. The unexamined life may or may not be worth living, but for me, life without a project is at best a shallow experience."

Thomas Moser was born in Chicago in 1935. His father, Josef, an Austrian immigrant, was a stereotyper responsible for assembling and aligning the curved lead plates from which the *Chicago Tribune* was printed. He was an artist in lead, a tradesman in the finest old-world sense. Sabina, Thomas's mother, was a German immigrant, hardworking and frugal. Both parents held a prodigious work ethic; they were ambitious and determined. A singular piece of advice consistently came to Tom from his father's spare speeches: "Buckle Down!" And Tom did, again and again.

Buckling down was no longer a choice when sadly Tom lost his mother when he was fourteen, then his father when he was eighteen. "I am not sure what is the worst age to be when a parent dies," Tom says, "but the age of fourteen, the age at which a child is rapidly transitioning to adulthood, must be close to it." No "remnant of hearth" remained after the death of both parents, and in an effort to find structure in his collapsed world, Tom quit high school and joined the Air Force in April 1953.

Much of Tom's military service was spent in Greenland, where he says there was nothing to protect and no one to guard against. After four uneventful years, he realized that he could forge a future only through education. As the son of blue-collar immigrants and a high-school dropout with abysmal grades, few were impressed with his academic potential. He was admitted to the State University of New York at Genesco solely because he was a veteran. Unexpectedly perhaps, Tom began a happy engagement with education in the liberal arts and sustained his nascent family by working nights tuning pipe organs. He came to understand that every phenomenon has a formulary, a thesis and antithesis, and he discovered books and experts and worlds that he had not realized existed. No day passed without a stunning revelation.

In 1957, his freshman year of college, Thomas Moser married Mary Wilson, his high-school sweetheart whom he had known since he was fourteen and she was twelve. She was, and remains, the most sympathetic and supportive person Tom has ever known. Together they built their first house, a four-room cottage, over the course of a summer. The process taught Tom that if you can toenail a twelve penny nail into a rafter, you can build a whole house, breaking the tasks in small pieces that become a collection of achievements. The process was joyous, paving the way for the rewards of risk taking. The house still stands, a testament to youthful enthusiasm and an exercise in focused effort.

Moser went on to graduate school at the University of Michigan and Cornell University, where he took his most memorable course ever: The History and Aesthetics of the Parthenon. In that course he learned that inspiring architecture and furnishings have historical antecedents and that lasting design is incremental, constructed upon the accumulated wisdom of legions of designers and builders who have come before. It is this tenant that threads through the work of Thos. Moser Cabinetmakers.

After receiving his PhD in speech communications and teaching at several universities, including one in Saudi Arabia, Tom moved his family to Maine in 1966, where he had secured a teaching position at the University of Maine in Orono. The following year he left Orono and accepted a job at Bates College in Lewiston. Tom loved Maine and teaching but the 1970s brought a laissez faire academic atmosphere that frustrated him. Although there were many rewards in teaching, not the least of which was the security of a tenured position while raising a family of four boys, Tom and Mary Moser made the decision in 1972 to take a leave of absence from Bates College and test the waters as furniture makers. Having spent many years disassembling and reassembling antiques as a hobby at home, they had developed an eye for aesthetic decision making. Tom and Mary decided they were willing to take a risk to fulfill a dream—they never turned back. In the spring of 1972, Thos. Moser Cabinet Maker (Maker became plural a few years later to acknowledge the growing community of craftspeople within the workshop) began in an old Grange Hall in New Gloucester, Maine, with an $8,000 loan, no discernible business plan, and an abiding love for all things made of wood.

LEGACY IN WOOD

Thomas Moser

With this book, I hope to convey the thinking behind the design choices I have made. I hope that woodworkers, artists, architects, designers, and those who simply like furniture will learn something from my sometimes painful experiences, as I have learned so much from others through the years.

But perhaps more than that I want to give some sense of the passion that keeps me still engaged in designing and building things out of wood. The joy of teaching the craft to others and observing their growth remains strong.

1

INFLUENCES

History will judge whether I'm a good designer, but I am certainly well-versed in traditional furniture design and construction. The library in which I write these words holds some one hundred volumes on the subject. I have read all of them, and many, many more that have slipped through my hands but remain in my unconscious. I have pursued and conversed with the modern masters of wooden furniture design, including Sam Maloof, George Nakashima, Hans Wegner, and innumerable others. I have taken apart hundreds of pieces of old furniture and then rebuilt them, trying to understand why they were made as they were. In restaurants, hotels, and the homes of friends, I have embarrassed my family countless times by crawling under tables, flipping over chairs, removing drawers, opening lids, prying back moldings, lifting mattresses, pursuing the backsides of cases, and generally looking shamelessly into the dark and hidden recesses of furniture both iconic and pedestrian.

Everything I have encountered and learned tends to impress itself upon our furniture as it moves from concept to reality. Perhaps this is part of the reason why, years ago, a friend called our work "historically ambiguous." Though offered in a humorous and offhanded way, her assessment was altogether accurate.

෨

I am undoubtedly influenced by nineteenth-century Shaker design. To me it is deeply mysterious that such masterful, graceful, even spiritual objects could have come from those largely unschooled people. Economy, utility, practicality, and proportion all merge into beauty that transcends culture and nationality. Indeed, I have discovered in my European and Japanese travels that Shaker design is as highly revered in those lands as it is in the United States. The impetus behind their works must, quite simply, have been a life force greater than those nineteenth-century craftsmen.

Non-Shaker American furniture pieces of the early nineteenth century—called country Chippendale, country Hepplewhite, or country Sheridan—influenced my work, as well as early eighteenth-century Queen Anne, with its curvilinear cabrial legs and cyma curves. All of these forms were, in turn, rooted in traditional English design, which is only logical; early American settlers brought their tools, skills, and tastes along with them from Europe as a whole, and from England in particular. Even today, if I had to link our furniture to any one tradition, it would be that of the skilled American nineteenth-century cabinetmaker—including the Shaker cabinetmaker—whose designs were rooted in utility, economy, and proportion and who used the wood at hand, locally sourced—never mahogany, teak, luan, or other rainforest lumber.

Another early influence was the work of John Ruskin. Ruskin's writing and art were precursors to the Arts and Crafts movement, which eschewed superfluous decoration and used joinery as ornament. In fact, Arts and Crafts workers sometimes intentionally deepened scribe marks, made joints self-consciously large, and installed hardware that was not just functional but oversized and rough hammered in iron or copper—all attempts at celebrating the work of the hand.

Design and structure should not occupy separate realms—much of an object's artistry should spring from the structure holding it together. This idea is radical but harkens to both the Shakers and Ruskin. With most furniture, in fact with most of the built world, all too often the purpose of design is to conceal structure. Historically, the structure of most furniture has been largely endoskeletal; that is, buried under the decorative skin, almost as if the joinery that held the piece together and made it work was an embarrassment. This design philosophy reached a high—or low—point in the flamboyantly veneered surfaces characterized by marquetry, where the point is not just to conceal the structure but to conceal the fact that the object is furniture. Hiding structure seems to me an affront to the craftsman. Furniture building is primarily an exercise in joinery. If the craftsman knows the finger joints, mortises, tenons, and other structural elements will be hidden, the temptation is strong to make them quickly and sloppily, resulting in furniture that works poorly and falls apart prematurely. Our furniture reveals and celebrates joinery, ensuring beautiful, well-crafted results, and thereby benefitting everyone.

Danish design, specifically that of the 1950s, moves toward a simplicity of form that came to be known as twentieth-century Danish Modern, and it is another significant influence on our work. Many Americans don't realize that such Danish masters as Hans Wegner, Borge Mogensen, and Arne Jacobsen were the first to discover, revere, and reinterpret American Shaker furniture. When I saw Wegner's Wishbone Chair—a stunning, minimalist design with its characteristic V-shaped back slat and other Danish interpretations of Shaker forms—I had an epiphany. From that moment on we began even more earnestly to do with our furniture precisely what the Danish had already done: reinterpret Shaker furniture for a modern sensibility. Aligned with the our aesthetic, the Danes also have an unmatched reverence for natural materials, even greater than that of the Shakers, who often painted their furniture.

The Danes believe, as I do, that wood is more satisfying than chrome plated steel or aluminum. Leather is more beautiful than plastic. Cotton, linen, and silk are superior to polyester. And oil and wax are far more appealing than polyurethane. Despite the proliferation of synthetic materials, I believe that human beings feel uncomfortable around them because we don't have a history with them, and consequently we don't understand them. They are mysterious, and we are hardwired to equate mystery with danger.

The longing for the natural materials with which we co-evolved is welded into our DNA, and as we alienate ourselves more and more from the cottage and the cave, our yearning for the natural world grows stronger.

I admire the German Bauhaus movement, the general term for the design philosophy of the Staatliches Bauhaus, an industrial arts school founded by the architect Walter Gropius in the Weimar Republic in 1919. The mission of the school was to bring the clean streamlined functionalism of the best of modern technology into the home. While I do not revere the school's choice of materials—the cold clinical chrome, steel, and glass of Bauhaus chairs, lamps, and other furnishings—I find the forms themselves satisfying in their minimalism. This same minimalism is evidenced in nineteenth-century Shaker case work and later in the Arts and Crafts contributions of Geritt Rietveld, who pays homage to Piet Mondrian.

The business of tracking down design influences can get dicey. Is there a common thread that unites the designs of Frank Lloyd Wright, German Bauhaus, Arts and Crafts, and the rest, and that also explains why we seem to instinctively find them appealing?

I think so, and the answer is nature herself. Nature is replete with economically engineered organic materials, and I believe each of my favorite schools of design attempts, consciously or otherwise, to replicate her feat. Function, not superfluous ornament, is the criterion by which nature designs. Even the outlandish colored markings of the male peacock or painted bunting serve a function.

The best furniture design considers first what the object must do.

If an object is functional, it is by definition beautiful as well. The best designs take nature for their inspiration; in fine woodworking, it is the common root, literally and figuratively.

2

AESTHETICS

What is the Moser aesthetic? I can usually recognize our pieces anywhere but I have never arrived at a shorthand label for our design philosophy. Others have termed it transitional, postindustrial, organic, minimalist, neo-Shaker, and, oddly enough, both traditional and contemporary. The best course might be to avoid categorization altogether, but since certain characteristics and influences of the Moser aesthetic can be pinned down, it seems worthwhile to attempt classification.

Every design we make is rooted in the basic preference for simplicity of form, precise craftsmanship, and respect for natural materials. If power corrupts, so can artistry. Fine woodworking has been characterized as the art of hiding mistakes, and that is too often true. Stains, paint, gilding, lacquer, and veneers are usually ways of concealing inferior design, workmanship, and or materials of dubious quality. An ancient Greek school of philosophy advocated sophistry, which celebrated deceit, making the worst appear the better, a principal not lost in most modern manufacturers of furniture. Too often what you see is not real wood or real joinery, but a shell, one-fiftieth of an inch thick, hiding fake wood and pocket screws. From the very beginning, we have dedicated ourselves to avoiding such concealment, but how does one take these fundamental personal preferences and translate them into furniture? A bedrock tenant of my aesthetic is that beauty is inseparable from inherent integrity.

Things are beautiful almost precisely to the degree that they celebrate their true nature.

So I am always loathe to stain, bleach, fume, paint, or otherwise artificially color any wood. Nature does that for us. Also, I believe that hidden structure flies in the face of human nature. Human beings want to understand the workings of the things they see. While we can endure the uncertainty of how things are made, the modern penchant for hiding structure leads, I think, to a mild neurosis.

Creativity, according to some, is synonymous with originality. Infused with divine inspiration, the artist should conjure objects ex nihilio, identifying general aesthetic preferences, and then dreaming up designs in an intellectual vacuum, unfettered by tradition. In the college level design courses I have taught, I found this attitude common. Students pay little or no attention to historical forms, apparently fearing their creativity might be stifled. I strongly disagree. The best designers are avid students of the history of design. They synthesize and improve, but they always work within a framework of forms that have existed for decades, even centuries. Just as the best novelist must first master the language, the best wooden furniture designer must first steep himself in a vocabulary of historic styles, joinery, proportion, wood species characteristics, finishing, and dozens of other arts, many of which were highly evolved centuries ago. Indeed the past is prologue to the future.

The processes of designing and building are impossible to tease apart. While designing by building is tedious and slow, the great advantage is that the tools and the wood become collaborators, constantly informing us of what will and will not work and actually suggesting ideas that we would never imagine if confined to a drawing board, or worse, a computer screen. Much brilliance results from historical accident or true serendipity. Most of all, I hope more and more people will regard themselves as neither designers nor builders, but both. It is from these people that the best designs have come, and will for eternity.

A piece of furniture—in fact, any created object—is a unique confluence of design, workmanship, and material; and each element bears responsibility for the success or failure of the whole. I consider the material to be the essential feature. Plastic, for example, has inherent qualities that suffer when it is made to look like wood or leather or any other organic material. Artifice, along with ornamentation, is meant to obfuscate. Plastic is a valid material and should celebrate itself, period.

It is utility that separates fine art from fine craft. The more useful an object the less art is ascribed to it. The visual artist creates two- or three-dimensional objects that exist purely to be looked at. Visual experience is the whole purpose of visual art and the mere notion of usefulness as a criterion for artistic excellence is deemed absurd. Indeed some argue that it is counterproductive. Oscar Wilde supposedly said that "all art is quite useless." Beyond the shock value, that statement is literally true. That is, fine art does not require an inherent use as does fine craft.

Unlike the visual artist, the craftsmen must produce two- or three-dimensional objects that serve practical human needs in addition to being pleasing to the eye. Moreover, the craftsman must produce physical durability and permanence in the work—two qualities not usually considered essential in fine art. There is a fundamental unfairness in all this. Since the beginning of recorded history acclaim has gone to the painter or sculptor, while the mason, woodcarver, or joiner has lived and died in relative obscurity. Why should finely crafted work made to serve humanity and endure the ravages of use not also be equally applauded for its aesthetic and cultural value?

Great design should be archetypal, giving the impression that adding, subtracting, or changing the proportions of any element would defeat its integrity.

Naturally, furniture design is not driven solely by style. The fundamental design criterion for any piece of furniture, particularly task seating, is the size and shape of the human body. It does not matter, for example, if the chair is Shaker, Chippendale, Danish Modern, or injection-molded Jetson plastic, the seat must be about eighteen inches above the floor and there must be roughly twenty-one inches between the arms. Furniture built in ignorance of or indifference to human body proportions will not work, no matter how carefully it is otherwise designed or crafted.

3

THE WINDSOR CHAIR—
MOSER STYLE

Experiencing a chair requires all of the senses.

A chair is first experienced visually, then tactilely, then kinesthetically—through the eyes, the hand, and finally the whole body. Some wooden chairs smell of wax and creak when sat in, so we can add olfactory and auditory perception as well. In building chair forms, it usually takes me four to eight total revisions before the chair is acceptable. Even then we must reserve the right, indeed the responsibility, to revise from time to time an angle here, a dimension there—even two or three years after the design has been "finalized." Designing and building a chair is a process of trial and error. As mistakes are corrected, a chair is born and reborn, and like scientific method, it is always subject to change.

In order to provide bodily support and comfort, a chair must meet at least five rules of design. First, since the chair is meant to be sat upon, it must accommodate the human body. This is no easy task since there is such a bewildering variety in human forms. Although some compromise is always in order, the designer is considerably limited in this regard. Second, pieces of furniture often serve in conjunction with something else, such as a table or a desk. Third, a task chair must be readily moveable. Fourth, because of the lightness, which enables the movement, the chair must flex with strain. And fifth, it must be pleasing to the eye.

A graceful chair design considers color, texture, visual movement, appearance of structural stability, balance, and symmetry. The successfully designed wooden chair should also exhibit some internal tension (what I call structural antagonism). A well-made chair should be sprung (able to give) and exist under tension in the same way a violin or piano is sprung by countervailing tensions. This tension can be heard. The spindles of a wooden chair can be played as a harp; where there is symmetry, pairs of spindles should vibrate at the same pitch. A task chair, while it may still fulfill the above criteria, is a tool for work and partners, typically, with a desk or table. A task chair is not built for relaxation, its center of gravity is forward and it must relate to another object that facilitates a function. On the other hand, a lolling chair has a center of gravity well aft of the seat.

Among all the variations on the Windsor chair, the Moser Continuous Arm Chair epitomizes for me what Plato termed ultimate "chairness," an ideal form. Form and function are inseparable. It is the closest thing to sculpture we can sit in while still functioning as essentially utilitarian. I am persuaded by long experience that there is more—or perhaps less, depending on how you look at it—to come in the perfection of seating. The chair that embodies transcendent "chairness" is a goal that recedes forever, and I don't believe I would have it any other way.

Of all the chairs we build, the Continuous Arm Chair is the most difficult to engineer, but also the most versatile. In 1975 we began experimenting with multi-ply laminates to form the distinctive arm. Early American arms were made of steam-bent hickory, ash, or oak, but lacked consistency of form. All of the components were quite simple to construct, but until we figured out the arm press, the early prototypes were clumsy at best. The Continuous Arm Chair as it has evolved is now about the eighth version of our original. Its form and function are inseparable. What has endeared Windsor chairs to many people has been their adherence to the principles of minimalism. This economy of form delights the eye much like a spider's web or finely tuned suspension bridge. One is not overwhelmed by mass or magnitude, as with architectural case furniture or a box frame chair, but rather the eye dances along delicate, straight, and curved lines connected only here and there at the point where they intersect the arm or seat. The emphasis is always on economy of material.

What we call the Windsor chair began in seventeenth- and eighteenth-century England but was really perfected in late Colonial America, in Philadelphia, Rhode Island, and Boston. While sack back, bow back, birdcage, and fan back chairs evolved in England, the Continuous Arm Chair is uniquely American. Over time our version of the Windsor, the Continuous Arm Chair, has seen several changes. The chair seat has been slightly deepened, two more degrees have been added to the back legs and rear spindles, a little more roll has been cut into the front of the seat and the arm terminus has been softened. We have been building the chair as it presently appears for several years and think it is in its definitive form. The ultimate criterion for chair design, however, is sustained and varied use.

Our most recent version of the Windsor, the Sequel to the Continuous Arm Chair, designed by my son, David, is an exercise in pure reduction. Both chairs inhabit the same space—one is constructed with "fragile" components, the other gains its strength through mass.

Our intent in all our designs is to eradicate ornamentation— to improve design by taking something away.

The progression of our Windsor chairs is an interesting metamorphosis illuminated by this Ruskin quote: "Nothing that lives is or can be rightly perfect, part of it is decaying, part nascent. In all things that live there are certain irregularities and deficiencies which are not only a sign of life but sources of beauty."

Another favorite concept of mine regarding sublimated ornamentation is the Japanese notion of *Wabi-sabi*. If an object or expression can cause within us a sense of serene melancholy and a spiritual longing, then that object could be said to be wabi-sabi. Wabi-sabi nurtures all that is authentic by acknowledging three simple realities: nothing lasts, nothing is finished, and nothing is perfect. Wabi connotes rustic simplicity, freshness, or quietness, and can be applied to both natural and human-made objects or understated elegance. It can also refer to quirks and anomalies arising from the process of construction that add uniqueness and elegance to the object. Sabi is beauty or serenity that comes with age when the life of the object and its impermanence are evidenced by its patina and wear. These ideas fit nicely into the Moser aesthetic and drive our enduring relationship with wood as well as the evolution of the Windsor chair.

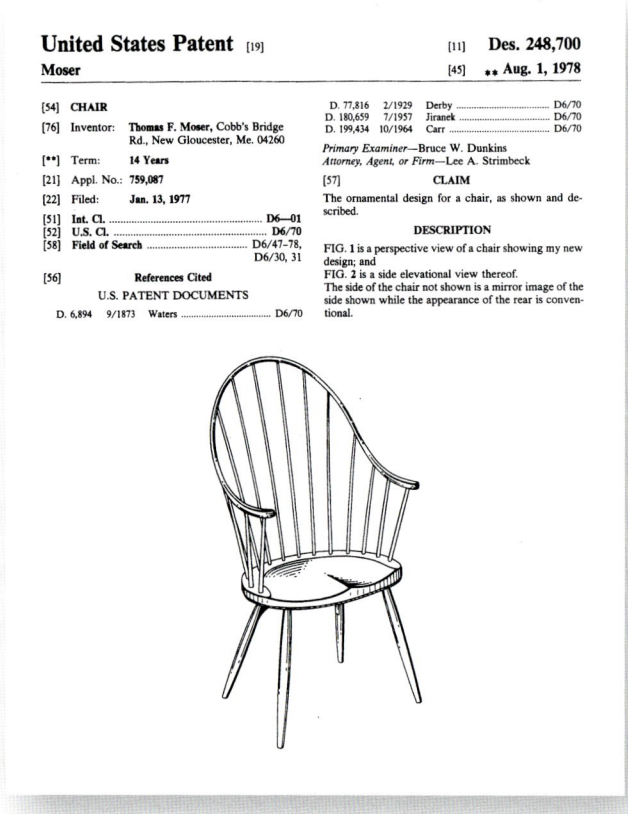

4

FROM THE FOREST

With rare exception, the furniture we produce is made of American black cherry. Despite my enduring admiration for this wondrous wood, we used very little in the early days because the species, *prunus serotina,* is not native to Maine. By 1976, with the evolution of an identifiable style, we began using black cherry—with ash for turned members—almost exclusively and have ever since. This is less convenient and more expensive than using native Maine wood, as it must be trucked more than five hundred miles from Pennsylvania, but we have never regretted the choice.

Why cherry? First and foremost, cherry is beautiful. Cherry has color, a term inadequate to describe the play of sunlight and shadow on a sanded, oiled, and waxed board. The wood has a unique translucence, evoking a reflecting pool rather than a simple mirror. The auburn hues ride not only on the surface, but also inside and they are visible as such. No other native American wood can rival this color and figure. More than any other wood, when finished it invites people to touch it. Perhaps this is some atavistic desire to be warmed by a campfire. Whatever the reason, after more than four decades, I still feel the pull and cannot pass without a touch.

Cherry is also highly workable. The wood is rich in resins, particularly prussic acid, that react rapidly to both ultraviolet light and oxygen, so cherry achieves in six months the patina that oak or maple acquire only after decades. Cherry machines extraordinarily well if you approach it respectfully. Due to the high concentration of volatile tannins, it burns easily, so woodworkers must use sharp tools, and keep the stock or the tool constantly moving. With cherry you cannot cheat in the sanding process, but must move from 80- to 120- to 220- to 400-grit to avoid scratch marks. Cherry is also difficult to steam bend; overheating turns it a singed purple. On the plus side, once dried to 6 to 8 percent moisture content, cherry is relatively stable, allowing us to make large panels important to our design.

All solid wood expands and contracts with changes in humidity and temperature. The expansion coefficient of cherry is 92 to 1. That is, it is stable along its length but subject to change across its width. Accounting for this phenomenon is central in designing furniture made of cherry, or any other solid wood. Accordingly, seams made in August are tighter than those made in February.

Cherry takes a non-membrane finish well, adapting more easily than some of the oil-rich hardwoods such as teak or open grained oaks. The use of any finish must always spring from respect for the material. Given that tenant, perhaps the most reverential finish for our work would be none at all. That is what many Scandinavian masters do with their finest pieces. On several trips to Denmark, and in discussions with the late Hans Wegner, a Danish national treasure and leading European chair designer, I discovered that the Danes best work is left unfinished. Pieces are maintained with an annual rubdown of steel wool or fine sandpaper. But the reality of modern life, and of the American market in particular, require some finish. Water on unfinished wood can irreparably stain it, so a life of Zen-like austerity is required to preserve the integrity of naked wood. Most people, myself included, cannot muster such a life.

So what kind of finish allows the greatest respect for the material? Most furniture receives a membrane finish, a more or less impermeable film such as paint, lacquer, shellac, varnish, or polyurethane. But if the film is ever breached—if it cracks, peels, yellows, or wears away, the underlying wood can be ruined by water. Varnish and polyurethane, along with other high-tech polmers, are subject to ultraviolet breakdown; they lose their sheen and turn milky. Cellulose lacquer, on the other hand, retains its "gin clear" transparency but breaks down from moisture and even moderate use, though catalyzed lacquer has improved this considerably.

Worst of all, membrane finishes are difficult to repair. When they are scratched, alligatored, or turn chalky, the only remedy is to strip away the entire finish and refinish the piece. Non-membrane finishes, that is oil finishes, are forgiving. A little fine sanding and a little oil applied to the area needing repair and the job is done. Practical considerations aside, whenever I see wood encased in a thick membrane I have a mental image of it suffocating. The time-honored method for treating a gunstock at the end of hunting season is to rub it briskly with boiled linseed oil to "case harden" the surface. Heat from hand friction lowers the oil's viscosity allowing it to penetrate. With an old walnut gunstock, a gorgeous luster and surface tension that repels water is the result. What is good for a gunstock works equally well for a tabletop. I realized that simple friction was not the only way to develop heat and began warming boiled linseed oil on a hotplate, experimenting with temperatures from tepid to hot. I discovered that oil warmed to about 130° penetrated wonderfully. While a drop of room-temperature oil would slowly and reluctantly soak into the wood, a heated drop vanished into it like melted butter on a cotton shirt or a silk necktie.

Finally, in 1976 we settled on the finish we use today. First, we polish the surface to a 400-grit finish. Then, using a spray gun or a soft cotton rag, depending upon the size of the piece, we apply a coat of 130° boiled linseed oil. We allow the oil to soak in for half an hour, wipe away the excess, then wait a day and rub the whole piece with Scotch-Brite, a synthetic abrasive equivalent to the traditional quadruple zero steel wool. In the case of tabletops, we may also rub down with a 400-grit wet and dry sandpaper. We repeat the process once more, for a total of two coats of linseed oil applied over four or five days. Finally, we rub on two coats of Butchers Bowling Alley wax, which is a mix of carnauba wax and beeswax, rubbing vigorously by hand with the grain.

This is an extraordinarily labor and time intensive finish, but the result is wonderful; the wood seems to come to life again. Polyurethane is tougher in the short term, but I have never found a more durable finish than ours in the long run. After about five years, the volatile elements of linseed oil have evaporated to leave the finish case hardened, like on that gunstock. You can set a sweating lemonade glass on it overnight and find nary a ring the next day.

Since we first started using cherry in 1976, the price has tripled for first- and second-grade cuts. Cherry has grown in popularity both in the U.S. and abroad—Europeans and Asians import millions of board feet of American black cherry each year—and its popularity worries me greatly. I fear the inventory of 70- to 120-year-old logs on which we depend will vanish in the decades ahead. The United States Forest Service believes that American black cherry is growing three times faster than it is being harvested. This is true in terms of bio-mass, but many of the large, mature trees are being replaced by scores of small saplings which will require over a century to mature.

Quite simply, cherry wood is so precious that it is a crime to make ugly or impermanent things from it. Our furniture is crafted to last for well over a century, but I believe some pieces, with care, could last five hundred years or more. That is a long horizon, but cherry deserves no less.

༃

The white ash and maple we use comes from Maine and New Hampshire. This region produces the finest northern hardwoods in the United States. Ash is used not only for it's contrasting color and texture, but also because its long fibers bend with pressure and afford comfort where most needed.

In recent years we have been using more and more black walnut. It grows best in an area from Ohio to Missouri. We source this beautiful, stable, and rewarding wood from midwestern river bottom land in Southwestern Missouri. Its dark color is enhanced by linseed oil and it achieves it permanent color immediately.

Black walnut's greatest attribute in design is its consistency in tone which celebrates form over surface activity.

Walnut is the favorite wood of Adam Rogers, who has taken the design reigns from David Moser in recent months. Adam studied architecture and design at Rochester Institute of Technology and is an accomplished furniture designer. His minimalist design is well suited to those whose predilection is largely contemporary.

Beyond efficiency, I believe our best conservation effort is to create the finest, most durable, beautiful, and timeless furniture that we can. Our intent is to serve generations not yet born while giving a tree a second life.

5

TECHNOLOGY AND THE HAND

Having more or less mastered hand tools and adopted the fruits of modern technology, I feel the various means of making furniture can be as interesting as the furniture itself.

British designer and architect David Pye, in his book, *The Nature and Art of Workmanship,* calls the kind of work we do, "the manufacture of risk." As he puts it, this type of manufacturing is characterized by "any kind of technique or apparatus in which the quality of the result is not predetermined, but depends on the judgment, dexterity, and care which the maker exercises as he works."

In other words, when you begin to work on a piece you are not exactly sure what the object is going to look like because you allow chance and choice to be part of the everyday production process.

Manufacturing becomes infused with humanity.

The pieces produced reflect how the craftsman felt the morning he or she pounded in the last wedge, or whether the board split when an operation was attempted, which then required sawing off half an inch and starting anew. When the worker spends fifty hours assembling a piece, literally thousands of challenges arise that require a reaction, and no two craftsmen will react the same way. This individualized and nuanced stamp of the maker is revered at Thos. Moser Cabinetmakers. In our shop, the introduction of technology will always be in service to the maker and will never overtake the authenticity of the hand.

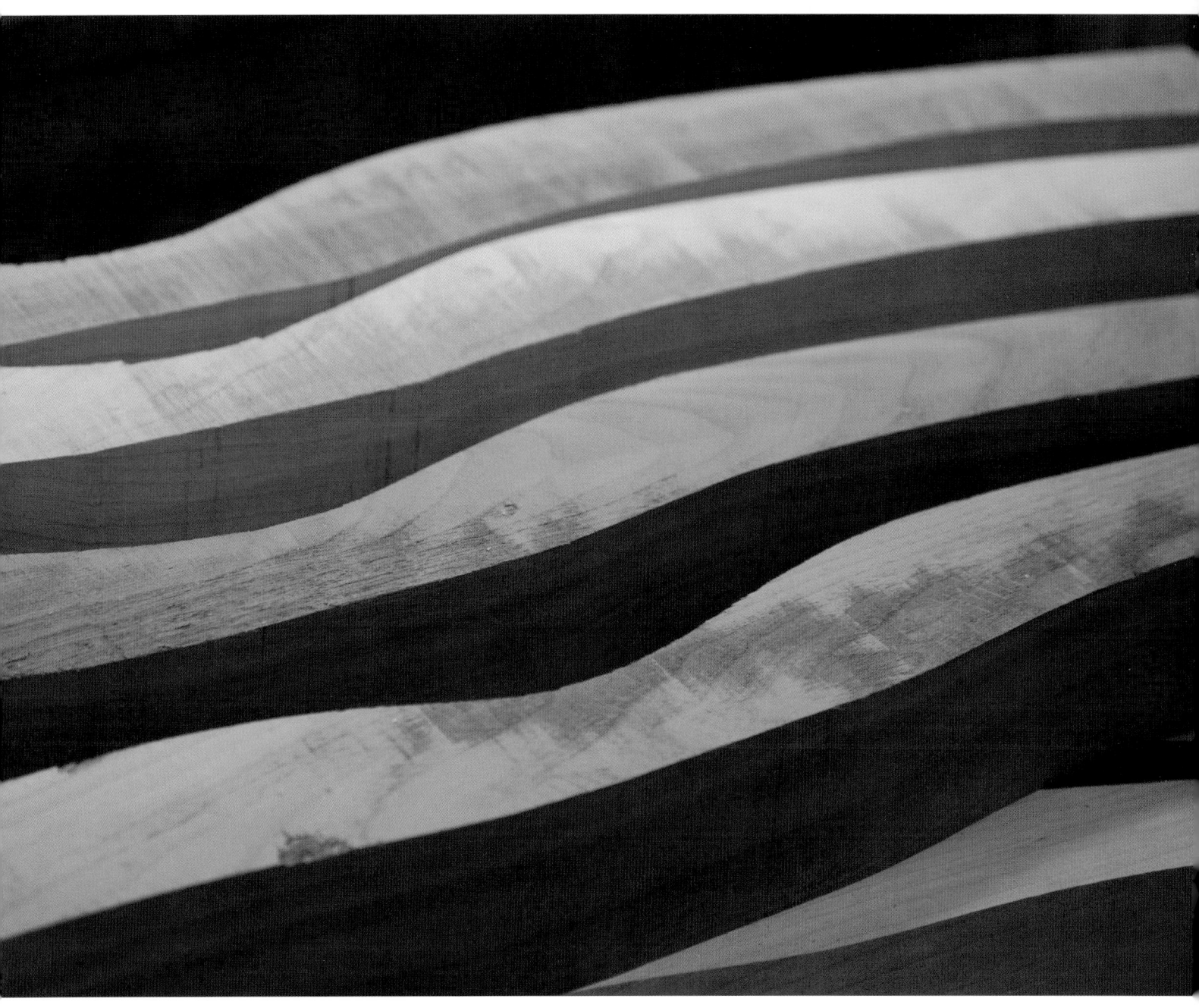

Most companies design furniture around the means of production to maximize machine efficiency and minimize the need for skilled manual labor, which is scarce and expensive. This is a slippery slope, however, that leads to inferior outcomes. History shows that the best furniture happens when the designer creates the finest forms he or she can, then adapts the means of production to accommodate that design. Typically, each piece of furniture can be cut, carved, curved, sanded, and finished by a variety of hand and machine tools. Joinery methods are legion. A corner, for example, can be dovetailed, butted, box joined, rabbeted, mitered, lock jointed, doweled, mortise and tenoned (a half a dozen kinds of mortise and tenon joints are possible), pocket screwed, biscuited, splined, and more. The curve in a round table's apron can be steam bent, flitch cut and glue laminated, or sawn from a wide plank. New woodworking technologies emerge seemingly every week, more and more tools are computer-controlled, and new cutting technologies such as lasers are replacing age-old metal blades.

How do we decide which method to use? First safety, then efficiency. Efficiency is, above all, conservation of time, humans' most precious commodity. We could theoretically use nothing but hand tools to produce our furniture, but prices would soon multiply, placing the furniture out of the reach of all but the extremely wealthy. Further, and importantly, the furniture would be no better. In some ways it would be worse. Instead we have always engaged in a delicate balance, seeking to find the best way to build a given piece that involves no compromise in aesthetics or structural integrity. The only synthetic we use on a continuing basis is polymerized glue, which replaces animal hide glue. Although our operations have evolved significantly over the decades, we have never made a change that sacrifices quality; and in every case a faster method was used only if the resulting product was as good or better than what it replaced.

6

CREATING A COMMUNITY OF MAKERS

Originally Thos. Moser Cabinetmaker was a family endeavor. The business started in our home, a 1780 Colonial in New Gloucester, Maine. My tools were in the cellar, where I designed and built all the furniture, and our dining room was our first showroom. Mary was my partner, my inspiration, and my administrator. In addition to keeping the books, selling the furniture, and marketing and advertising the work, she also managed the affairs of our four young boys. After school, each of our sons had chores to do in the shop.

Gradually I incorporated apprentice students from Bates College, paying them fifteen dollars a day. I hired my first non-student employee, Ed Boyker, in 1974. He was fifty-three years old, an accomplished finish carpenter of the old school who had spent most of his lifetime building interiors for wealthy, demanding mill owners in the area. Ed was self-taught and could build anything of wood, from barn roofing to high-end urban shelving to wooden shoe lasts. I have acquired a tremendous amount of knowledge from Ed and other skilled artisans with whom I have worked with through the years. For example, it fascinated me that Ed did virtually no measuring, working instead with "story poles," scraps of wood on which he marked crucial dimensions to determine spacings. He could build a complex and precise piece of furniture while having almost no idea of any of its dimensions in inches or feet.

In the summer of 1972, with two students from Bates College, we built our first "line" of furniture. The line consisted of reproductions, mostly from furniture at the Shaker Village at Sabbathday Lake, Maine, along with some pieces from Colonial Williamsburg, Virginia, and Sturbridge Village, Massachusetts. By 1975, a subconscious worry suddenly surfaced. I realized that what we had produced was largely imitative and that did not bode well. Whose equity were we enhancing? Many of the designs we were building had been created by men who had been dead for a hundred and fifty years. We were enhancing their stature, not our own.

There and then, I determined that we needed to create our own definitive style.

This was a risk, of course, and we had to sell our house to pay off debts and underwrite the business.

The creation of what has become our style had more than an economic impetus. I also had a strong sense that the best design is simple, unadorned, and in harmony with the material. I very much wanted to build on the traditional furniture forms with those values in mind.

My oldest son, Matthew, soon became my number one lathe operator. His turnings were beautiful and found their way into many early designs. Matt worked at my side all during our startup years. After a hiatus of several years working in antique restoration in Portland, Maine, Matthew returned to work at Thos. Moser in both Auburn shops for sixteen years before opening his own design/build company in New Gloucester. Matt eventually moved to San Francisco, where he designs interior fixtures and corporate offices.

Our second son, Andrew, also worked summers and after school as a shop apprentice. After serving in the Air Force, he worked along the waterfront in coastal Maine building marine structures. The work was physically demanding and after falling off a number of wharf construction sites into the North Atlantic, particularly in winter, he returned to the shop in 1987, where he has worked in a number of areas including the rough mill, furniture assembly, chairs, and repairs.

Because our furniture sells at the high end of the market, for many there is a natural resistance to make that first purchase. To overcome this we recently developed a small line of accessories such as treasure boxes and candle holders. These are not only less expensive, they are made to inventory and therefore can satisfy gift giving. Using as much scrap wood as possible, Andrew is not only responsible for producing these small items, he is using scrap wood that would otherwise be burned in the wood stove.

Aaron, our third son, also worked after school stacking lumber, doing maintenance and generally making himself useful in the early years. As a graduate of the Culinary Institute of America, Aaron apprenticed in Boston and New Orleans and became a master chef in Dallas, supervising a crew of forty. A chef works long and strange hours and after his children were born, he and his wife Lisa—who met Aaron while working as our IT manager—decided that returning to the Moser fold would be a reasonable course. In 1991 Aaron joined the company and was responsible for two major expansions of the shop. He also took over the sales and administration of our contract division that had begun five years earlier, realizing that this was an area that was ripe for inspired quality furniture. Contract furniture is non-residential, for such places as offices, courtrooms, and libraries. In the twentieth century, domestic furniture had become imitative, uninteresting, and cheaply made (now mostly Chinese made). Quality and innovation was occurring in contract furniture spurred by the designs of Hans and Florence Knoll, Mies van der Rohe, Le Corbusier, Ero Sarrinen, Charles and Ray Eames, Herman Miller, and others. This became an exciting arena for us as well.

Of our four sons, Aaron is by far the most tenacious and has developed admirable sales skills and organized major non-residential installations, particularly academic libraries. Aaron has installed Thos. Moser furniture in many offices and libraries nationwide (see appendix) and his efforts account for about 20 percent of our revenues.

After college, our youngest son, David, spent his Peace Corps time in the mountains of Kenya. He returned to Maine in February 1989, and joined the family business. No one in the company has held more positions than David. Starting in the showroom, he was given the task of creating a customer survey. Soon his efforts turned to marketing and in time he became our marketing director, designing and building our showrooms in New York, Freeport, Maine, San Francisco, and Charleston. In many ways David is the most creative of our sons. Even as a little boy he was forever drawing and making fanciful paper and clay objects. Why he majored in economics remains a mystery, but then, his father's wanderings in life did not follow a prescribed path either.

In addition to the family, and after hiring Ed Boyker and the Bates College students, I hired Chris Becksvoort, a graduate of the University of Maine School of Forestry, who was from Silver Spring, Maryland. Chris's father was a German cabinetmaker who taught him the art and craft of handwork and imbued in him a reverence for finely made hand tools. This passion transferred to everyone in the shop. Thos. Moser Cabinetmakers continues to owe a debt to the discipline Chris brought to the making of furniture. Today Chris is a significant contributor to *Fine Woodworking Magazine* and has taught fine woodworking and hand craftsmanship nationally. Chris continues to serve as an advisor to the Sabbathday Lake Shaker Community in New Gloucester.

The last of the early non-family trio was Bill Huston, who left his father's cast iron foundry in Xenia, Ohio, to study fine woodworking in Norway, for two years before coming to us. Bill brought European joinery techniques and a passion for self improvement. He eventually became shop foreman. Today Bill operates his own business in Kennebunk, Maine, partnering with his son and employing several others.

∾

By the early 1980s we had thirty employees, including a number of college-educated apprentices who used the experience as a stepping stone in establishing their own one-man shops. These folks found themselves elbow to elbow with working-class people from Maine mill towns like Lewiston, Auburn, and Mechanics Falls, a social admixture of individuals who each served as a reality check for the other.

They include fine craftsmen such as Doug Green, who went on to secure a master's degree from Pratt in industrial design and mount his own successful furniture making company in Portland, Maine; Stuart Wurtz, whose workshop is in the Pacific Northwest; David Rogers, who has a master's degree in city planning from the University of Pennsylvania and has an architectural design firm in Auburn; David Vigneron, who majored in anthropology at Harvard and has his own business in the Berkshires of Massachusetts; Bob Newton, a successful Denver attorney who left the practice for five years to learn the trade before setting up his own shop in Yarmouth, Maine; Kevin Rodel, whose book on Arts and Crafts in America is recognized as seminal in the genre; and James Becker, Dartmouth graduate and a firecracker of a guy who was with us for six years and now builds furniture for Dartmouth College and many of its professors.

Thos. Moser Cabinetmakers is unique among woodworking operations in that we hire large numbers of women. Most Scandinavian shops I have toured, for example, have no female floor workers at all, but roughly 30 percent of our crafters are female. Although there are many exceptions, I have found that women are generally more patient and more detail oriented than men, and are consequently a great asset in final detailing. But the fact is, they can excel anywhere. For eight years, a woman ran our machine room, and had twenty-three people, all men, reporting to her. Forty-three years ago women were not found pulling lumber and running heavy-duty woodworking machinery. Along with other occupational roles this changed during the "back to nature" upheaval of the 1970s. Now there is nothing to bar women from the production floor. They build furniture alongside men—no project is too complex or demanding and Thos. Moser Cabinetmakers benefits from their fearless commitment.

By 1987 we had outgrown our second shop and therefore added an addition. But by 1990 it became clear that we needed still more space than the old Grange Hall afforded even after the significant expansion. In addition to space, we needed three phase power, better transportation infrastructure, and a more diverse work force. All this led to our buying an antiquated meat packing plant in Auburn on the Androscoggin River. The 21,000 square feet were on three floors and each floor was covered by six inches of concrete to accommodate cold storage. The task of demolishing the interior and reconfiguring it fell to David Moser. Over time we've expanded to the comfortable, efficient 65,000-square-foot shop we occupy today.

Rounding out the team, in August 1995, Harry Fraser, a seasoned executive, was hired to serve as CEO and remained for thirteen years. He was succeeded several years later by Bill McGonagle our current CEO, who has helped return us to financial stability. His contribution and leadership has undone damage from the recent recession and we are once again whole.

To solidify a sustained Moser aesthetic, Adam Rogers was promoted by Thos. Moser Cabinetmakers in 2013 to director of design and product development. Before joining the company in 2010, he received his master's degree in furniture design and woodworking at RIT. Prior to graduate school, Adam received an undergraduate degree in architecture and spent a number of years as a designer in corporate architecture. Studying woodworking solidified his commitment to the respect for craftsmanship, fostered his understanding of and reverence for wood, and helped him establish a sensitivity for the role of subtlety and nuance through simplicity and detail. The designer recalls, "I realized I was lacking the personal relationship to my work that I genuinely yearned for when working in architecture. My goal remains to have a connection with the object, from concept through realization, and to marry craft to the design process…. The world isn't in need of more objects. Turning trees into furniture is a responsibility." Adam is altruistic regarding furniture design, applying, as did Thomas Moser, a true respect for the history of furniture to products of increasingly modern appearance.

Adam views the Mosers as woodworkers—listening to the material to arrive at a shape, instead of starting with a function or a visual vocabulary. He states that his aesthetic is different from Tom's and David's, but is based on the same principles: respect for wood, elevation of craft, and simplicity of form. Interpretations of those principles will continue to evolve with culture, context, and the perspectives of additional designers. Adam feels strongly that "the reasons why we make furniture are pure, the way we craft the furniture is honest, and our ability to manufacture is world-class. Thomas Moser started this company in 1972 with the mission of restoring the lost art of woodworking, and of creating a community of craftspeople who could support themselves doing work they believed in while creating objects of true value for customers. This remains a noble mission and one that I support wholeheartedly."

Adam Rogers's talents are receiving accolades nationwide from such entities as *Metropolis*, *Contract*, and *Interior Design* magazines.

Having established a woodworking shop in our new space we needed to staff it with dedicated craftspeople whose desire to work balanced their lack of experience. The new folks came to us because they simply needed a job, whereas the New Gloucester contingency had a longer, career focused outlook. Accordingly, we had two shops, one for the alternate lifestyle aspirants and the other for folks who needed a paycheck and loved to work with their hands. Our sons Matthew and David were instrumental in keeping the two enterprises productive. As time passed the New Gloucester folks left in pursuit of their own business ambitions and production gravitated to old meat packing plant in Auburn.

By the late 1990s David and I worked closely together designing and prototyping new pieces. It was not always a smooth process—it seldom is among fathers and sons—there were disagreements, but each of us made efforts to consult the other as we proceeded. By 2002, David was increasingly responsible for new product design, including the development of the American Bungalow collection, often with little or no input from me. His work tends toward the curvilinear, the complex, and the more contemporary. Mine is, as a friend once said, more Germanic—straight lines and square corners. Both design preferences prove relevant and have been well received in recent years.

Without the unselfish effort of Mary and the boys, Thos. Moser Cabinetmakers would not exist in any meaningful form. Not only did they offer emotional support, but each in their own way brought us to where we are today.

I learned design and construction techniques from people who've been dead a hundred and fifty years or more. That is, I've taken apart furniture that was built in the eighteenth or nineteenth century and reconstructed it. I think that is called reverse engineering. I deduced or inferred how they did things. The craftsmen in our shop mostly came to us, with the exception of Bill Huston, with limited formal training, but were all well intentioned and wanted to learn the craft. As a teacher and a self-taught woodworker, I learned a long time ago that readiness is essential in the teaching and learning of a person—child, adolescent, or adult—and these folks arrived "ready."

Traditionally, craftsman in the past several hundred years apprenticed to a master craftsman, and did not achieve journeyman status until later. Starting in the early days of Thos. Moser Cabinetmakers, once sufficiently skilled, the craftsman who built a piece of furniture from woodpile to finished piece signed his or her work. We signed on a little scrap of paper that was glued to the piece as it might have been done in 1800. We soon learned that this was not a good approach and began to use India ink penned onto the wood itself. On every piece you will see Thos. Moser Cabinetmakers, Auburn, Maine, and then the signature of the maker and the year. There were times early on when people thought this idea was a chore, but it didn't take long for them to realize that they were given an opportunity to put their name on something that would live long after they were gone. There are precious few opportunities in contemporary American life where you can put your name on something that your great, great, great grandchildren will see. There is a level of pride in that. I know there is no such thing as immortality, but it's nice to know that the work you've done is going to give pleasure and meaning and utility long after you fade away.

Even among the whirling blades and hissing pneumatic clamps in our shop, a good eye and a fine aesthetic sensibility are crucial. Our workers choose the lumber that will go into an individual piece, and they must possess a keen appreciation for how to match color and grain for an overall pleasing effect. It is not unusual for the selection of lumber for a single piece to take longer than its assembly. The skilled, time-consuming matching we practice is one of the biggest contributors to the beauty of our work.

The trust that we place in the individual craftsperson is so high that every worker also functions as an inspector, the final arbiter of excellence, empowered to pull a piece out of line for repair or replacement if he or she spots an imperfection. This tenet means that group pride rather than oversight from above becomes the primary motivator and condition for quality control. It gives agency to the community of craftsman at Thos. Moser Cabinetmakers and instills them with the pride that arises from making something with a lifetime guarantee. I owe a debt of gratitude to every craftsman in our shop, as they have taught me much over the years.

A few words from the early crew at Thos. Moser Cabinetmakers:

BILL HUSTON

Tom and Mary created an environment where not only beautiful, heirloom quality furniture was being built, but it was being marketed in a way that the business was sustainable and the craftsmen made a decent living. During those years in the late '70s, Tom assembled a group of very intelligent, highly skilled craftsmen. Almost everyone was college educated and the lunch-hour discussions around the wood stove were intense—sometimes going on for two hours. It was an amazingly creative group that fed off one another and we all grew in many ways because of it. Bringing that talented, inspired group together was one of Tom's and Mary's early achievements.

ELIZABETH WHELAN

There are three things that stand out when I look back at my experience working with Tom. First, there was a sense of materiality. Each morning when I entered the showroom in Portland, I was greeted by the scent of linseed oil and cut wood (the custom shop was behind the showroom in those days). I still love that smell, it is the scent of materials in the making. For some reason, I have a great curiosity for different materials: traditional and non-traditional. I believe being around objects in which the material itself is a significant factor influenced my fearlessness of material.

Second, I made good friendships at Thos. Moser Cabinetmakers that lasted through the years. They were formed at the walnut dining table in the back of the showroom. There was a lot of humor and lively discussion at lunch every day. To this day, I take my lunch at a round table in my studio with my staff. We just get a chance to know each other a little better.

Third, I grew to love furniture. I learned to flip it upside down, look at the way it was made, and evaluate styles, materials, and aesthetics. This familiarity with furniture has been an important asset to my development and growth as a designer. I have teamed up with other furniture designers, most notably Niels Diffrient, for fifteen years, designing textiles for his very advanced ergonomic chairs, where function and performance were as important as aesthetics.

DOUG GREEN

It was 1981 when Tom Moser asked me to come work in his nine-year-old furniture business. I had been making furniture in my own little shop in Topsham for several years but jumped at the exciting opportunity to learn from master woodworkers. The workshop was still at the old Grange Hall in New Gloucester, where I was one of six cabinetmakers and, by far, the least experienced. It was a continuous learning experience and I loved the intensity and passion every member of that community held for the values and practice of traditional craftsmanship.

While absorbing the cabinetmaker's sensibility, I began to invent new jigs to speed up repetitive tasks and found that I had an innate ability to search for ways to eliminate wasted effort and improve efficiency. Bill Houston, who was managing the shop, was astounded that after only six months, this rookie had become the most productive cabinetmaker at the shop. Discovering my knack for design and problem solving, I decided to enroll in the Pratt Institute Industrial Design program, graduated, and returned to Maine to start my own company, Green Design.

I will always be grateful to Thos. Moser for giving me the opportunity to discover that I was an inventor.

DAVID VIGNERON

During my first years among the eight to ten Thos. Moser Cabinetmakers, I sometimes felt I was in a lobster tank of egos. Self-confidence and satisfaction were necessary, but an absolute sense of superiority seemed excessive. While my fellow employees each fit into a different category of personality, we all shared one drive. We suffered for the art of perfectly executed traditional furniture manufacture. The high quality of the workshop environment, the fine material, and especially the variety of designs Tom sold, all maintained our interest and accentuated the sensation of performing a unique occupation at a singular time. Tom is known for his gregarious conversational manner, and arguments always seem to go his way. He previously succeeded as a professor managing demanding college students. This surely prepared him to guide his furniture makers' egos in a productive direction. Though he was a very flexible employer, opinion on the shop floor held that, should you refer to yourself as a designer within Tom's earshot, you would be well served to bring your jacket home with you that night. Yes, the largest ego belonged to Tom himself! I eventually came to realize the inflated egos were justified; and, furthermore, knowing you're the best at something is essential to success.

KEVIN RODEL

I started work at Thos. Moser in 1979. It was the perfect job for an aspiring young furniture maker—somewhat like an Old World workshop experience but with modern equipment. I had my own bench and built each order from start to completion, except for the finishing. Each day presented a new problem to solve, there was little routine except for Tom's lunchtime yarns. After seven years in that small New Gloucester shop I learned to be efficient, precise, and flexible; good attributes for venturing out on one's own.

Thos. Moser Cabinetmakers Customer in Residence program officially launched in September 2007, when five long-time Moser customers spent a week with us here at our shop in Maine building furniture and staying in Freeport's historic Harraseeket Inn. What started as an experiment has blossomed into a full-fledged residency program that has attracted interest from all over the globe. To date, 300 people from 40 states, plus England and Canada, ranging in age from 16 to 84 and from all backgrounds, have participated in this fulfilling adventure. They are paired with a master crafter and at week's end return home with a finely crafted piece of furniture.

People from all walks of life come to Maine in the summer to partake in the residency program: doctors and dentists, who work on every part of the human body and mind; engineers, who design everything from tiny semiconductors to huge aircraft carriers, sports stadiums, and solar fields; scientists, who are researching everything from new drugs to continental drift; architects and designers, including a retired Disney imaginer and a designer from the car industry; academics, who teach everything from economics and lean manufacturing to ballet; business people, from Fortune 500 companies down to smaller entrepreneurial ventures; people from the legal and law enforcement world, including a judge, an FBI agent, and a state trooper; government employees, including a retired CIA official and a former secretary of the treasury; and people who protect the country, including a Navy Seal who was recently made admiral, as well as veterans of all branches.

What do they all have in common? Regardless of what they do in their professional lives, they are very successful. However, the product of their labors is not something they can bring home with them to use and enjoy for the rest of their lives and then pass down to their children. Even if they are amateur woodworkers, they have difficulty finding the time to build large projects, improve their skills, and share the craft. The Customer in Residence program gives them an opportunity to test their skills in a fully equipped shop with a master craftsperson available for consultation and assistance. It is a universally satisfying experience.

EPILOGUE

The Five Values

In the courtyard of the Bodleian Library at Oxford are seven doorways, each marked by one of the seven liberal arts. These disciplines are the bedrock of Western civilization. Our company also firmly established a foundation of values—five in number.

1. The furniture is our raison d'être; it is paramount in all our thinking. We strive always for excellence in materials, design, and execution.

2. The craftsmen and managers who build, sell, and administer our enterprise are the community responsible for our continued success. Their security and individual aspirations are of importance each day.

3. The customers who support our efforts by providing financial means for us to continue underwrite all that we do. That almost half of what we make goes into homes and offices that already contain Moser furniture is a testament to the worthiness of our efforts.

4 Efficiency in the use of both natural and human resources is ubiquitous. There is morality in efficiency. "Waste not, want not" is more than a quaint saying, it is ever present in our pursuit.

5 Financial profitability is the residue resulting from all of the above.

While these five values are listed in order of importance, they are coexistent. Remove any one and the rest becomes just a house of cards.

AFTERWORD

Donna McNeil

It has been a distinct honor and pleasure to work with Thomas Moser in assembling the exhibit "Legacy in Wood" at the Maine College of Art. I trust that it is as much of a joy to experience through these pages as it was to assemble. Tom's creativity, intelligence, wit, and enormous patience were a gift to me. He remains a great teacher. I am indebted to Thos. Moser Cabinetmakers and the Maine College of Art for the opportunity, to the staff for their support as I added to their workload, and to Mary Moser for nourishing me on so many levels—indeed, behind every successful man . . .

APPENDIX I

TIMELINE OF KEY MILESTONES

1972
Tom Moser takes one-year leave from Bates College without pay to make a go at furniture making. He never returns.

1972
Thos. Moser Cabinet Maker formed in February. Family dining room used as showroom. First year sales are $17,000.

1973
First ad in *Down East* magazine–sales double.

1975
Church vestry is moved to become first showroom, freeing up Moser's dining room.

1977
Original Moser designs introduced–Bow Back Chair, Corner Cupboard, TMC Rocker, Continuous Arm Bench, Dr. White's Chest.

1978
Tom's first book, *How to Build Shaker Furniture,* is published.

First ad appears in *The New Yorker*.

1981
First professionally designed catalog is published.

Shop moved to old meat-packing plant in Auburn—finally, three-phase power.

1982
Matthew Moser joins Thos. Moser Cabinetmakers.

Tom publishes second book, *Thos. Moser's Windsor Chairmaking*.

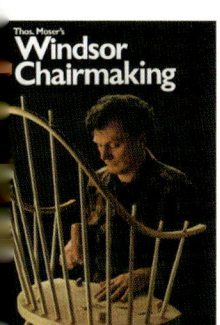

1983
Moser Contract Furniture, Inc., established.

1983
Eastward Side and Arm Chairs.

1984
First major showroom opens in Portland.

Maine Astral Bench wins The Hardwood Institute's Daphne Award for Design Excellence in Designer/Limited Production Furniture and an award from the Institute of Business Design (IBD).

New Gloucester Rocker.

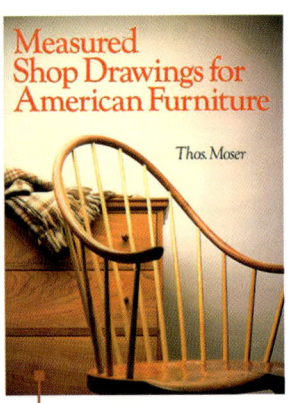

1985
Thos. Moser's *Measured Shop Drawings* published.

Chandler Chair National IBD Gold Award for Sectional "Racetrack" Conference Table.

1986
High Stool.

1987
Andrew Moser joins the company.

New shop completed on current site. New Gloucester and Auburn consolidated.

Philadelphia showroom opens.

Thos. Moser Cabinetmakers launches company-owned delivery operation.

Companion Manufacturing Company (toys) formed.

1988
Library furniture introduced: Reader's Chair, Washington Square Chair, Writing Desk (8- and 4-leg), Slant Top Desk.

Storage Chest.

Blanket Box.

Low Post Bed.

RJK Bed.

1989
David Moser joins the company.

1990
Alexandria, Virginia, showroom opens.

1991
Aaron Moser joins the company and is placed in charge of nonresidential sales.

Thos. Moser Cabinetmakers is one of 200 companies to be named a Blue Chip Enterprise by the U.S. Chamber of Commerce, *Nation's Business* magazine, and Connecticut Mutual Life Insurance Co.

New Century Collection: Book Table, Book Desk, Book Shelf, Round Stand Twenty, Side Table w/ Shelf, Round Table Forty, Coffee Table Penta, China Bed, Study Carrel, Square Extension Dining Table.

Thos. Moser Cabinetmakers makes seven custom gallery benches for the Reagan Presidential Library in Simi Valley, California.

1992
San Francisco showroom opens.

Courtroom Side and Arm Chairs.

Harpswell Side and Arm Chairs.

Healthcare Collection Rocking Chair wins IBD New Product Award.

1993
New Century Collection: Arm and Side Chairs, Side Board, Slat Bed, Pedestal Extension Tables, Square and Round, Hannaford Hutch, Acadia Side Chair, High Rocker, New Generation Rocker.

Manhattan showroom opens on Madison Avenue.

1994
Philadelphia showroom relocates to Walnut Street, in the historic heart of Center City.

1995
Windward Collection: Lounge Chair, 2- and 3-Place Sofa, Dining Chair, Bookcase, Coffee Table, Square Coffee Table, Glove Table, Bench.

1996
18,000 square feet added to the shop.

In collaboration with Futaba Kogyo Co., Thos. Moser furniture is displayed and sold in Japan.

Thos. Moser Cabinetmakers is one of two companies (LL Bean is the other) profiled in the state's annual report as best exemplifying the Maine image.

1998
Katahdin Collection: Side and Arm Chairs, Stool.

Lolling Collection: Chair, Ottoman, Side Table, Sleigh Bed, Bates Chair.

Freeport, Maine, showroom opens.

HANDMADE AMERICAN FURNITURE

1999
Franklin County Chair.

Crescent Collection: 4-Drawer Dresser, 6-Drawer Dresser, Dressing Box, Dressing Cabinet, Wardrobe, Dressing Glass, Stool, End Table, Sofa Table.

Island Collection: Side Chair, Arm Chair, Tablet Chair.

2000
Sofia Collection: Chair, 2-Place and 3-Place Sofas, Studio Couch, Chaise, Four Poster Platform Bed.

2001
Chicago and Charleston showrooms open.

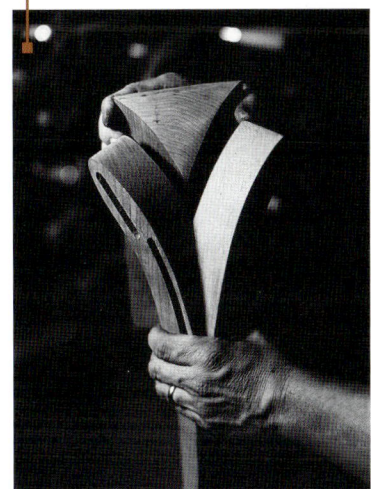

2002
American Bungalow Collection: Round Extension Table, Square Extension Table, Dining, Sideboard, Open Sideboard (originally called a book case), Dining Side and Arm Chairs, Lounge Chair and Ottoman, 3-Place Sofa, Coffee Table, Sofa End Table, Bookcase.

Thos. Moser's *Artistry in Wood* published.

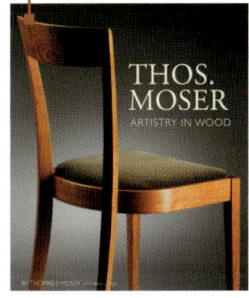

2003

Catena Arm and Side Chairs.

Crescent Sideboard.

Newport Dining Chair.

Georgetown Single- and Double-Pedestal Tables.

Island Bed.

Fireside Bench.

Washington, D.C. Showroom opens in Georgetown's Caddy Alley.

American Bungalow Collection: Bed, 7-Drawer Dresser, Dresser with Doors, Wing Chair and Ottoman.

2004

Wing Collection: 2- and 3-Place Sofas, Corner Cupboard w/ Glass, End Table, Hall Table.

Chicago Showroom relocates to historic Tree Studios at North State Street.

American Bungalow Collection: 2-Place Sofa, Club Chair, Rocker, Double Square Extension Table, 2-Drawer File Cabinet.

Bowfront sideboard reintroduced.

Boston Show Room opens.

Canterbury Collection: Cupboard, Four Drawer Chest, Seven Drawer Chest, Bracket Base, Courtroom Stools, Game Table.

Player's Chair reintroduced. Built for a string quartet, it has an adjustable seat.

Vertical File Cabinet.

Chef's Table.

Oval Ring Coffee Table.

Thos. Moser Cabinetmakers brings on two associate showrooms in Columbus, Ohio, and Seattle, Washington.

2005

Vita Collection: Chair, Ottoman, Side Table, Coffee Table.

Crescent Collection: Hutch, Display Case, Georgetown, Cafè Table, Occasional Table.

Thos. Moser Cabinetmakers wins the "Best Maine Small Family Business" Award and the Blue Chip Enterprise Award from Connecticut Mutual, the U.S. Chamber of Commerce, and Nation's Business.

Vita Collection: Lounge, Credenza, Étagère, Museum Bench.

Aria Collection: Dining, Side, and Arm Chairs, Dining Extension Table, Sideboard.

Wing Collection Occasional Table.

Another 18,000 square feet added to the Auburn shop.

2006

Inverted Arm Chair reintroduced.

Aria Collection: Dressing Table/Writing Desk.

Vita Collection: Bed, 2- and 3-Place Sofa.

Newport Swivel Chair.

Edo Collection: Trestle Table, Dining Chair, Studio Chair, Bench, Café Table, Stool, Coffee Table, Hall Table, Side Table, Round Dining Table, Open Sideboard, Sideboard with Doors, Lounge Chair, 2- and 3-Place Sofas, End Table, Stool.

Tivoli Collection: Chair, Ottoman; 2- and 3-Place Sofas.

2007
Shaker Grandfather Clock reintroduced in limited edition.

Hawthorne Arm and Side Chairs.

Vita Collection: 3-, 6-, and 9-Drawer Dressers; Dining Table and Chair.

Tivoli Collection: Upholstered Lounge Chair, Ottoman, Sofa.

American Bungalow Collection: Writing Desk, Filing Cabinet, Wing Club Chair, and Ottoman.

Edo Trestle Table wins Spark Awards Gold.

Hawthorne Chair wins Spark Awards Silver.

First Customer in Residence session is held.

2008
Pasadena Collection: Dining Table and Chair, Hall Table, Aria Stool.

Los Angeles showroom opens.

Astral Bench reintroduced for residential sale. Per Borre design reengineered by Thomas Moser.

Edo Collection: Rocker, Cantilever Side Table, Wing Round Coffee Table with glass.

Pasadena Dining Chair wins "Best of Year" award from *Interior Design* magazine

Pasadena Collection: Slipper Chair, Ottoman, Sofa, End Table , Occasional Table, Coffee Table, Bremen Table, Chine, Chaise, Perry Screen.

2009
Kinesis Chair and Ottoman.

Pasadena Rocker.

Pasadena Rocker wins "Best of Year" Award from *Interior Design* magazine.

Meridian Collection: Dining Chair, Rectangular Dining Table, Sideboard, Hall Table, Small Chest with Doors/Drawers.

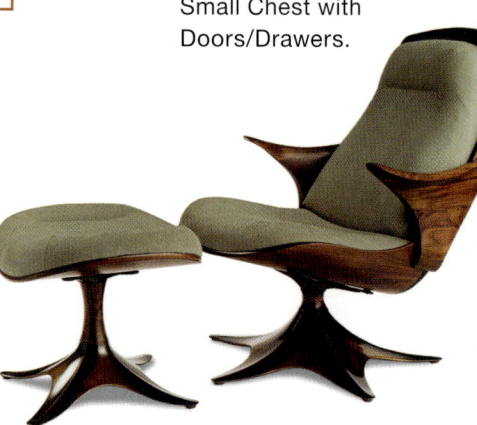

2010
Edo Bed.

Meridian Collection: Stool, Coffee Table, Round Dining Table.

New Harbor Lounge Chair and Ottoman.

2011
Drift Lounge Chair and Ottoman.

Thos. Moser Cabinetmakers named Best Furniture Maker in *Down East* magazine's "Best of Maine" and Best Furniture (Wood, Transitional) in *Boston* magazine's "Best of Boston."

Ellipse Collection: Dining Chair, Dining Table, Sideboard, Stool.

Philadelphia showroom (Wayne, PA) opens.

2012
Vintage Collection: Reintroduction of vintage pieces for 40th anniversary, Shaker Peg Mirror, Storage Bench, Grange Hall Table, Ellipse Collection, Lounge Chair, Ottoman, Sofa, Coffee Table, End Table, Media Case, Sideboard with Doors, Bed, Dresser, Side Table.

American Bungalow Collection: Armoire, Bookcase, Mirror.

Castine Collection: Dining Table and Chair, Sideboard.

2013

Hunt Chair, designed by Aaron Moser for North Carolina State University in honor of Govenor Hunt.

Element Collection launches at NeoCon and is the first collection designed by a non-Moser. Wins a Best of Neocon Silver Award from *Contract* magazine.

Thos. Moser Cabinetmakers named Best Heirloom Furniture in *Boston* magazine's "Best of Boston."

Crescent High Stool. Thomas Moser inducted into New England Design Hall of Fame (*New England Home* magazine).

Element Collection receives Product Innovation Award from *Architectural Products* magazine.

Alienation Bench receives Award of Merit at Crafts Forms 2013, the 19th International Juried Exhibition of Contemporary Crafts in Philadelphia.

Adam Rogers named director of product design and development–the first non-Moser to oversee product development.

2014

Rockport Dining Table and Chair. Currently, this is my favorite chair. David designed it about two years ago.

Fahmida Chair wins a honorable mention Best of Year Award from *Interior Design* magazine.

Element Collection: Desk, Bookcase, Credenza.

Pacific Chair (Adam Rogers) launched at NeoCon in June. Wins a Metropolis Likes Award from *Metropolis* magazine and Best Products of the Year Award from *Design Journal*.

Cumberland Collection (Adam Rogers) is launched. Wins Best of the Year Award from *Interior Design* magazine.

Thos. Moser Cabinetmakers again named Best Heirloom Furniture in *Boston* magazine's "Best of Boston."

Thos. Moser Cabinetmakers wins Pine Tree Award from Maine Wood Products Association.

APPENDIX II

INSTITUTIONAL CLIENTS

Since 1984, a significant part of our business has come from applying our aesthetic to creating furniture for libraries and other public institutions.

Atlantic City Public Library

Episcopal School of Dallas

Dallas Hall of State

Baker & McKenzie

Elizabethtown College

John Jay College

The New Yorker magazine

Haverford College

Mount Holyoke College

New York Philharmonics Archives

Prince George's County Law Library

Williams & Connelly

Kilpatrick Townsend & Stockton

Indiana University–Purdue University Indianapolis

Kutztown University

Missouri State Library and Archives

Spokane Public Library

Catholic University of America

Seton Hall University

Burlington County College

The Lawrenceville School

Rockridge Branch Library

East Carolina University

Williamsburg Foundation

California Institute of Technology

Multnomah County, Oregon

Sidwell Friends School

St. Catherine's School

University of Dayton

University of Texas at Dallas

Phoenix Central Library

Thoreau Institute

Berkeley Public Library

Clark County Public Library

College of Wooster

Dallas Public Library

Dickinson College

Georgetown College

Harvard University

Indiana Historical Society

Muhlenberg College

West Town Middle School

Yale University

Institute for Advanced Studies

International Tennis Hall of Fame

New Jersey City University

University of Colorado

Agnes Scott College

Episcopal School of Dallas

Delaware State Archives

West Bloomfield Public Library

Boston Latin School

University of Wisconsin

Vassar College

Yeshiva University

University of North Carolina

San Diego Natural History Museum

Sandusky Library

Gutman Library

Thompson Library

Albert Einstein College of Medicine

Robert B. House Undergraduate Library

Webster University

Columbia University

George Washington University

New York University

Orland Park Public Library

University of Southern Maine

Duke University

Scranton Public Library

North Carolina State University

Arizona State University

DC Public Libraries

Salt Lake City Library

St. John's University

Vinalhaven Public Library

Fayetteville Public Library

University of Southern Maine

Darien Public Library

Samuels Public Library

Episcopal High School

Heritage Hall

Mamaroneck Public Library

New England Institute
of Technology

St. Bernard Parish Library

Avenues: The World School

Shorter University

University of Georgia
Special Collections

St. Timothy's School

Princeton Theological Seminary

Quinnipiac University

Ridgefield Library

George W. Bush
Presidential Center

Brown University

Emory University

Gunston Day School

Harvard Chemistry Library

King County Library System

North Pole Branch Library

Pace Academy

Gill Library

Fairwood Public Library

Reed College

Syracuse University

The Frick Collection

UCLA School of Law

University of Pennsylvania

City of Williamsburg

Belmont University

FURTHER READING

Andrews, Edward Deming, and Faith Andrews. Religion in Wood: A Book of Shaker Furniture. *Bloomington: Indiana University Press, 1966.*

Andrews, Edward Deming, and Faith Andrews. Shaker Furniture: The Craftsmanship of an American Communal Sect. *Albany: University of the State of New York, 1937.*

Andrews, Edward Deming, and Faith Andrews. Work and Worship among the Shakers: Their Craftsmanship and Economic Order. *New York: Dover Publications, 1982.*

Becksvoort, Christian. The Shaker Legacy—Perspectives on an Enduring Furniture Style. *Newtown, CT: The Taunton Press, 2000.*

Chippendale Thomas. The Gentlemen and Cabinetmakers Director. *Original publication 1754. Mineola, NY: Dover Publications, Inc., 1966.*

Goyne-Evans, Nancy. American Windsor Chairs. *New York: Hudson Hills Press, 1996.*

Hepplewhite, George. The Cabinetmakers and Upholsterer's Guide. *New York: Dover Publications, 1794.*

Kassay, John. The Book of American Windsor Furniture. *Amherst, MA: University of Massachusetts Press, 1998.*

Kirk, John T. American Furniture. *New York: Harry N. Abromson, Inc., Hudson Hills Press, 1966.*

Maloff, Sam. Woodworker. *Tokyo and New York: Kodansha International, 1988.*

Meader, Robert F. W. Illustrated Guide to Shaker Furniture. *New York: Dover Publications, Inc., 1972.*

Moser, Thomas. Thos. Moser's Windsor Chairmaking. *New York: Sterling Publishing Co., Inc., 1982.*

Moser, Thomas. Measured Shop Drawings for American Furniture. *New York: Sterling Publishing Co., Inc., 1985.*

Moser, Thomas. How to Build Shaker Furniture. *Cincinatti, OH: Popular Woodworking Books an imprint of F & W Media, Inc., 2011.*

Moser, Thomas, with Brad Lemley. Artistry in Wood. *San Francisco, CA: Chronicle Books LLC., 2002.*

Nakashima, George. The Soul of a Tree: A Woodworkers Reflections. *Tokyo and New York: Kodansha International, 1981.*

Nutting, Wallace. Furniture Treasury. *New York: The Macmillan Co., reprint 1962.*

Pye, David. The Nature and Art of Workmanship. *Bethel, CT: Cambium Press, reprint 1995.*

Rodel, Kevin P., and Jonathan Binzen. Arts and Crafts Furniture from Classic to Contemporary. *Newton, CT: Taunton Press, 2003.*

Santore, Charles. Windsor Style in America. *Philadelphia, PA: Running Press, 1987.*

Sheraton, Thomas. The Cabinet-Maker and Upholsterer's Drawing Book. *Mineola, NY: Dover Publications, Inc., 1791-1797.*

Sloane, Eric. A Reverence for Wood. *New York: Frank and Wagnalls, 1965.*

Sprigg, June. Shaker Design. *Scranton, PA: Norton & Co., 1988.*